Essential Question
What can you see in the sky?

Little Blue's Dream

by Daniel Haikin
illustrated by Anette Heiberg

The little blue bird stretched to see the great night sky. The stars twinkled.

"Mama, why are the stars so bright?" Little Blue asked.

Mama Bird said, "The full moon is sleeping. That makes the stars easier to see."

"When I fly, will I touch the stars?" Little Blue asked.

Mama Bird said, "No, the stars are too far away."

4

"My dream is to fly to the stars," said Little Blue.

"It's time for bed now," Mama said.

STOP AND CHECK

What are Little Blue and Mama talking about?

5

Mama Bird fell asleep. But Little Blue was awake! She started to climb the tree.

She jumped through tree branches. She leaped to the top. But the stars were still too far away!

The wind blew. Whoosh!
Another puff blew poor Little
Blue out of the tree!

She yelled, "Help! I'm
falling!"

Little Blue flapped her wings.

Mama bird said, "You're not falling! You're flying!"

STOP AND CHECK

What is Little Blue doing?

9

"Part of your dream is to fly," said Mama Bird.

"I did fly, didn't I?" Little Blue chirped.

Little Blue fell asleep. She dreamed she flew very high. She touched the stars with her wings.

STOP AND CHECK

What happened in Little Blue's dream?

Respond to Reading

Retell

Use your own words to retell *Little Blue's Dream.*

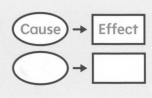

Text Evidence

1. Look at page 6. What causes Little Blue to climb the tree?

   Cause and Effect

2. Look at page 8. What causes Little Blue to fly? Cause and Effect

3. How do you know that *Little Blue's Dream* is a fantasy? Genre

Hello, Little Dipper!

Genre Nonfiction

Compare Texts
Read more about the night sky.

You can use a telescope to see stars.

There are a lot of stars in the sky. Most stars are very far from Earth. They are always there. The sun is a star. We can only see it during the day.

The Little Dipper is
made up of seven stars.

Some groups of stars make
shapes in the sky. These
shapes have names. The
Little Dipper is one of these
shapes. The stars of the
Little Dipper make a dipper
shape. It looks like a big
spoon in the sky!

Make Connections

Look at both stories. What did
Little Blue see in the sky? What can
you see in the sky? Text to Text

15

Focus on
Science

Purpose To find out what can be seen in the sky

What to Do

Step 1 ▶ Tell what you can see in the night sky. Write a list.

Step 2 ▶ Draw a poster to show what you can see.

Step 3 ▶ Talk about your poster. Tell what it shows.

Conclusion What can you see in the night sky?